Animal Noses

By Connor Stratton

level 2
little blue readers

www.littlebluehousebooks.com

Little Blue House is distributed by North Star Editions:
sales@northstareditions.com | 888-417-0195

Produced for Little Blue House by Red Line Editorial.

Photographs ©: iStockphoto, cover, 4 (bottom), 7 (top), 7 (bottom), 10–11, 12, 15 (top), 16–17, 18, 20–21, 23 (top), 23 (bottom), 24 (top left), 24 (top right), 24 (bottom left), 24 (bottom right); Shutterstock Images, 4 (top), 9 (top), 9 (bottom), 15 (bottom)

Library of Congress Control Number: 2020900793

ISBN
978-1-64619-179-6 (hardcover)
978-1-64619-213-7 (paperback)
978-1-64619-281-6 (ebook pdf)
978-1-64619-247-2 (hosted ebook)

Printed in the United States of America
Mankato, MN
082020

About the Author

Connor Stratton enjoys spotting new animals and writing books for children. He lives in Minnesota.

Table of Contents

Noses and Nostrils

Many animals have noses.

Noses help animals smell.

Noses have nostrils.

Some noses are large.

Other noses are small.

Noses can be
different shapes.
Some noses look
like stars.
Other noses look
like leaves.

Some animals have
only nostrils.
Birds have only nostrils.

Colors

Noses can be

different colors.

Some noses are black.

Some noses are pink.

Pigs have pink noses.

Mice have pink noses too.

Some noses are
pink and blue.

Long Noses

Elephants have
long noses.
Elephant noses are
called trunks.

Chameleons can have long noses.

nose

chameleon

Tapirs can have
long noses.
Anteaters can have
long noses too.

Glossary

anteater

elephant

chameleon

pig

Index